# PEREGRINE FALCON

**JOSH PLATTNER**

CONSULTING EDITOR, DIANE CRAIG, M.A./READING SPECIALIST

**Super Sandcastle**

An Imprint of Abdo Publishing
abdopublishing.com

# abdopublishing.com

Printed in the United States of America, North Mankato, Minnesota
062015
092015

THIS BOOK CONTAINS
RECYCLED MATERIALS

Editor: Liz Salzmann
Content Developer: Nancy Tuminelly
Cover and Interior Design and Production: Anders Hanson, Mighty Media, Inc.
Photo Credits: Shutterstock

**Library of Congress Cataloging-in-Publication Data**
Plattner, Josh, author.
 Peregrine falcon : master of speed / Josh Plattner ; consulting editor, Diane Craig, M.A./reading specialist.
     pages cm. --  (Animal superpowers)
 Audience: K to grade 4
 ISBN 978-1-62403-738-2
1.  Peregrine falcon--Juvenile literature.  I. Title.
 QL696.F34P55 2016
 598.9'6--dc23
                          2014048273

Super SandCastle™ books are created by a team of professional educators, reading specialists, and content developers around five essential components—phonemic awareness, phonics, vocabulary, text comprehension, and fluency—to assist young readers as they develop reading skills and strategies and increase their general knowledge. All books are written, reviewed, and leveled for guided reading, early reading intervention, and Accelerated Reader™ programs for use in shared, guided, and independent reading and writing activities to support a balanced approach to literacy instruction.

# CONTENTS

# BRILLIANT BIRD

Peregrine falcons
are large birds.
They are taller than
12 inches (30 cm).
Their **wingspans**
are 40 inches
(102 cm). They are
about the size of
crows.

# WHAT DOES PEREGRINE MEAN?

*"PEREGRINE" MEANS "WANDERER" IN LATIN.*

# FIERCE FLIER

What is this animal's superpower? Speed! Peregrine falcons are the fastest birds in the world. They fly more than 65 miles per hour (105 kmh). Sometimes they dive after their **prey**. Their diving speed is more than 200 miles per hour (354 kmh).

**160 MPH (257 KPH)**
AVERAGE HELICOPTER SPEED

**200 MPH (322 KPH)**
PEREGRINE FALCON DIVING SPEED

**230 MPH (370 KPH)** TOP FORMULA ONE CAR SPEED

# WORLD WANDERER

Peregrine falcons live all over the world. They live on six of the seven **continents**.

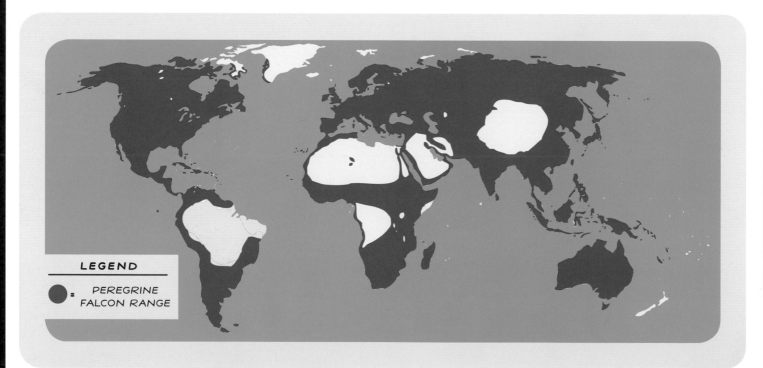

LEGEND

● = PEREGRINE FALCON RANGE

They like to live on coasts. In winter, they like to live in South America.

# HUNTING WITH HUMANS

People train peregrine falcons to hunt. It is called falconry. The human is called a falconer. Falconry has been around for more than 4,000 years!

# MIGHTY MARKINGS

Adult peregrine falcons are blue-gray. They have dark heads. Markings on their heads look like sideburns.

AN ADULT PEREGRINE FALCON

Young falcons have streaks.

The streaks go up and down.

Adults have stripes.

The stripes go side to side.

# DARING DIVES

Peregrine falcons hunt smaller birds. They can spot **prey** from 3,000 feet (914 m) in the air.

# STOOPING

They dive and strike at very fast speeds. This is called stooping.

# GUTSY GIRLS

Female peregrine falcons are larger than males. They are more powerful.

MALE PEREGRINE FALCON

FEMALE PEREGRINE FALCON

The males find a few places to make nests. The females choose which is best.

# NEAT NESTS

Peregrine falcons build nests. They collect **materials** to use. Their nests hold three to four eggs. Both adults care for the young.

# BYE-BYE BIRDY

Peregrine falcons used to be **endangered**. A **chemical** called DDT killed many birds. Today, there are more falcons than ever.

# FALCON SUPERHERO

Can you imagine a peregrine falcon superhero? What would it look like? What could it do?

# WHAT DO YOU KNOW ABOUT
# PEREGRINE FALCONS?

1. A peregrine falcon's superpower is speed.

TRUE OR FALSE?

2. Female peregrine falcons are smaller than males.

TRUE OR FALSE?

3. Peregrine falcon nests hold three to four eggs.

TRUE OR FALSE?

4. Peregrine falcons were never **endangered**.

TRUE OR FALSE?

ANSWERS: 1. TRUE 2. FALSE 3. TRUE 4. FALSE

# GLOSSARY

**CHEMICAL** - a substance made or used in a science experiment. Also, a substance made by chemistry.

**CONTINENT** - one of seven large land masses on earth. The continents are Asia, Africa, Europe, North America, South America, Australia, and Antarctica.

**ENDANGERED** - having few left in the world.

**MATERIAL** - something that other things can be made of, such as fabric, plastic, or metal.

**PREY** - an animal that is hunted or caught for food.

**WINGSPAN** - the distance from one wing tip to the other when the wings are fully spread.